THIS BOOK BELONGS TO:

HISTORY OF THE CHINESE ZODIAC:

THE CHINESE ZODIAC CONSISTS OF TWELVE ANIMAL SIGNS, BASED ON THE CHINESE LUNAR CALENDAR. THE MOON'S CYCLE REPEATS ITSELF EVERY TWELVE YEARS WITH TWELVE ANIMALS IN THE HOROSCOPE ASSOCIATED WITH ONE OF THE FIVE ELEMENTAL SIGNS: WOOD, EARTH, FIRE, WATER, AND METAL.

THE ORIGIN DATES BACK A FEW THOUSAND YEARS. ONE LEGEND IS THAT BUDDHA HELD A RACE TO DETERMINE WHICH OF THE ANIMALS WAS THE FASTEST. THE FASTEST ANIMAL WAS ASSIGNED TO THE FIRST CYCLE OF THE MOON AND SO ON. THE RESULT OF THE RACE WAS: ZI RAT (FASTEST), CHOU OX, YIN TIGER, MAO RABBIT, CHEN DRAGON, SI SNAKE, WU HORSE, WEI SHEEP OR GOAT, SHEN MONKEY, YOU ROOSTER, XU DOG, AND HAI PIG (SLOWEST).

A CHILD BORN IN THAT YEAR WOULD HAVE SIMILAR CHARACTERISTICS AND PERSONALITY TRAITS OF THE ANIMAL ASSIGNED TO THAT YEAR. ITS ALSO BEEN DETERMINED WHICH ANIMALS ARE COMPATIBLE AND WHICH ONES TO AVOID. FOR EXAMPLE, A RAT SHOULD STAY AWAY FROM HORSES, AND AN OX SHOULD AVOID GOATS. BUT A RABBIT WOULD BE COMPATIBLE WITH A GOAT OR PIG.

IN CHINA, BIRTH DATES ARE NOT AS IMPORTANT AS THE YEAR IN WHICH A PERSON IS BORN. IT'S CALLED HIS OR HER BEN MING NIAN. IF YOU WANT TO KNOW THE AGE OF A PERSON, DON'T ASK HOW OLD THEY ARE, ASK FOR THEIR CHINESE ZODIAC ANIMAL.

THE CHINESE NEW YEAR BEGINS AT THE NEW MOON WHICH FALLS BETWEEN JANUARY 21ST AND FEBRUARY 20.

1. WHICH ANIMAL REPRESENTS THE YEAR YOU WERE BORN?

2. WHICH ANIMAL STANDS FOR THE CURRENT YEAR?

1. PRINT THE CHINESE ANIMAL SYMBOL BELOW THAT
REPRESENTS FOR YOUR BIRTH YEAR.

2. SAY YOUR ANIMAL NAME IN CHINESE?

COMPLETE THE MAZE FOR THE
CHINESE LANTERN.

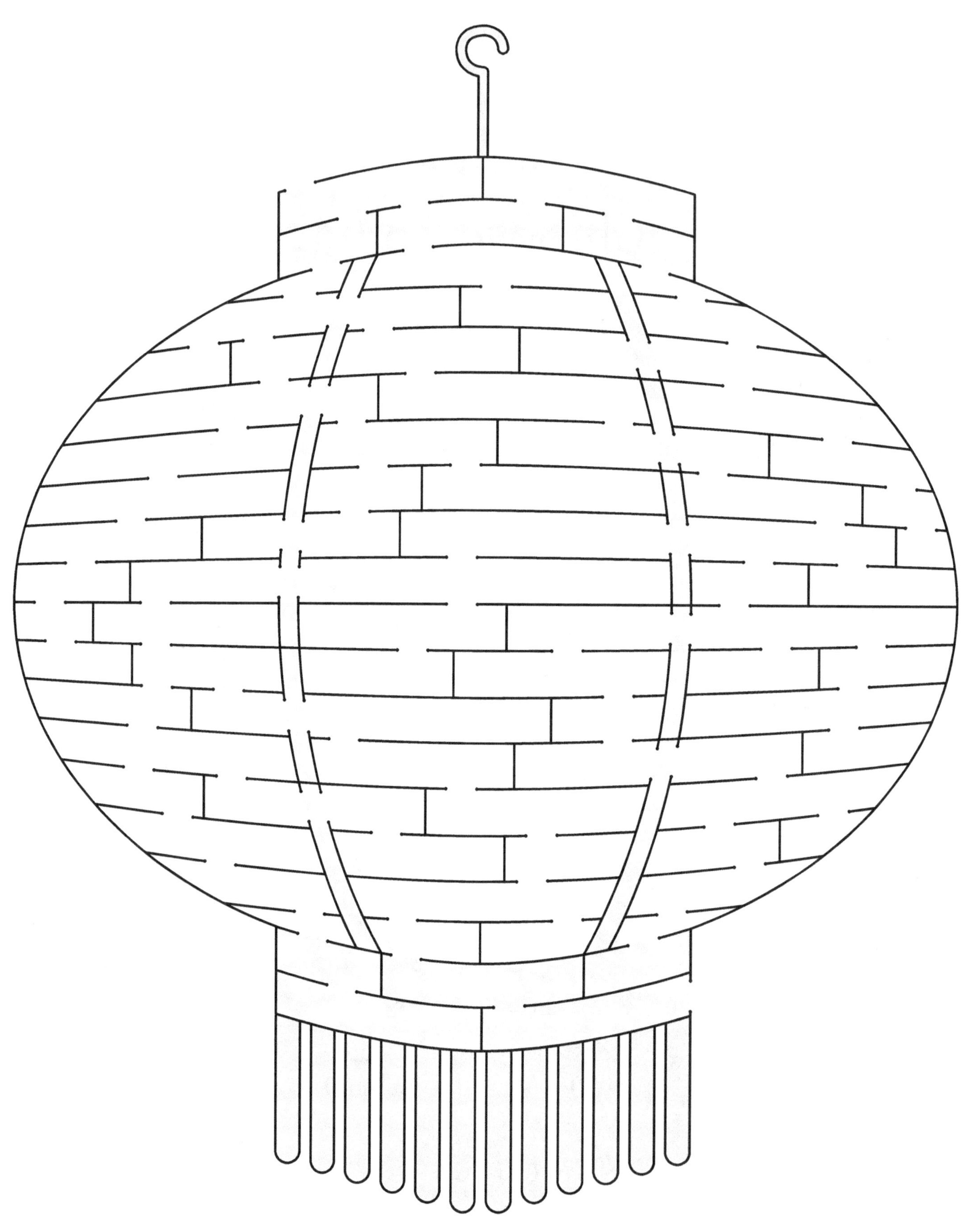

鼠
牛
虎
兔
龙
蛇
马
羊
猴
鸡
狗
猪

RAT

YOU ARE CHARMING, AMBITIOUS, PICKY, AND BRIGHT.

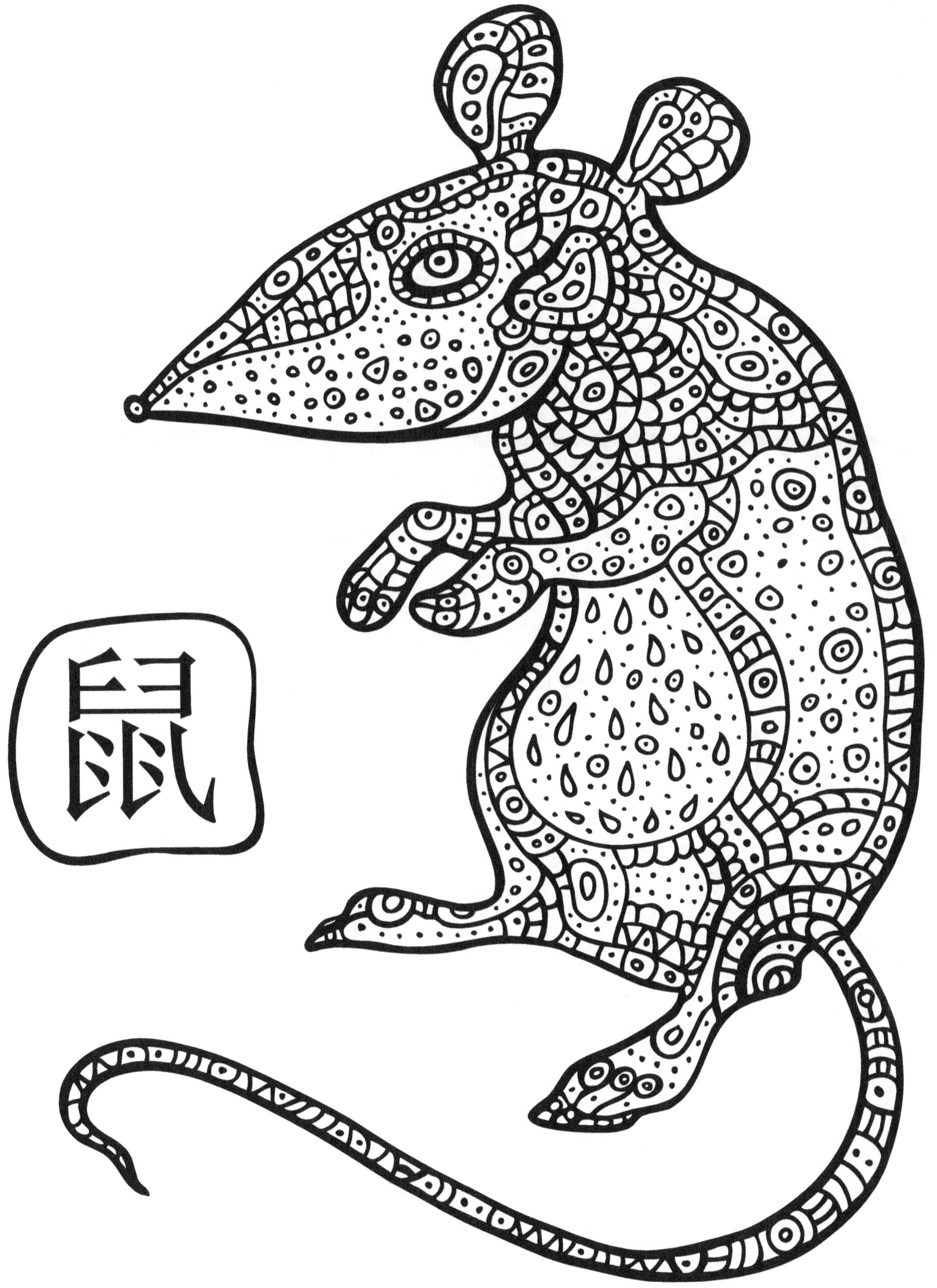

鼠

BULL or OX

YOU ARE PATIENT, DEPENDABLE, HARDWORKING, AND TRUSTWORTHY.

牛

TIGER

You are courageous, aggressive, powerful, and protective.

虎

RABBIT

YOU ARE KIND, AFFECTIONATE, VIRTUOUS, AND CONSIDERED THE LUCKIEST OF ALL THE CHINESE ZODIAC ANIMALS!

DRAGON

YOU ARE POWERFUL, WISE, WEALTHY, AND ENERGETIC. IT IS A GREAT HONOR TO BE BORN IN THE YEAR OF THE DRAGON!

龙

SNAKE

YOU ARE DETERMINED, INTENSE, PERSISTENT, AND VERY WISE.

蛇

HORSE

YOU ARE ATTRACTIVE, POPULAR, FUN-LOVING, AND ENERGETIC.

GOAT or SHEEP

YOU ARE CREATIVE, ELEGANT, TENDER, AND SYMPATHETIC.

羊

MONKEY

YOU ARE INTELLIGENT, CHARMING, INVENTIVE, AND AMBITIOUS.

猴

ROOSTER

YOU ARE INDEPENDENT, INTELLIGENT, ORGANIZED, AND VERY SOCIAL.

鸡

DOG

YOU ARE SINCERE, LOYAL, TRUSTWORTHY, AND VERY FRIENDLY.

狗

PIG

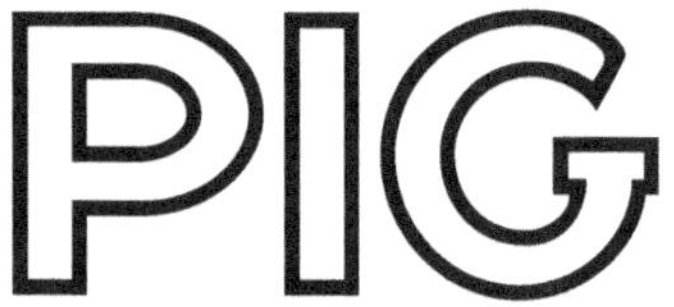

YOU ARE BRAVE, CHIVALROUS, NOBLE, AND MAKE LIFE-LONG FRIENDS.

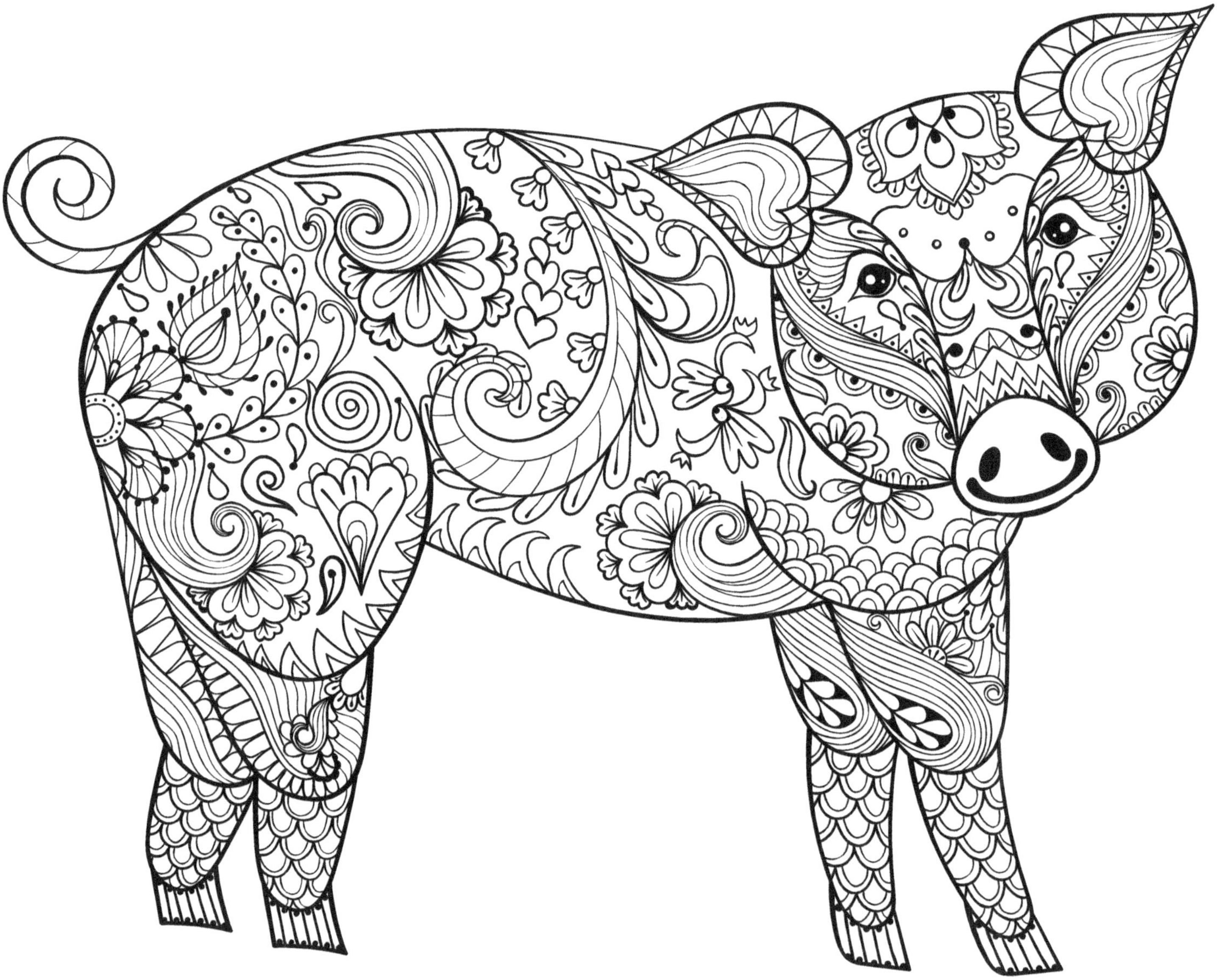

猪

COLOR THESE FUN
CHINESE ZODIAC
ANIMALS!

COLOR THESE FUN
CHINESE ZODIAC
ANIMALS!

COLOR THESE FUN
CHINESE ZODIAC
ANIMALS!

WHICH ANIMAL IS YOUR FAVORITE?
RESEARCH YOUR ANIMAL AND WRITE A FEW
FACTS ABOUT IT. FOR EXAMPLE, MY
FAVORITE ANIMAL IS A HORSE. HORSES ARE
PLANT EATERS (HERBIVORES). THEY CAN SLEEP
LYING DOWN OR BE STANDING. HORSES CAN
GALLOP AROUND 27 MPH (44 KPH).

WRITE AT LEAST TEN WORDS THAT YOU CAN MAKE FROM THE WORD CHINESE? HINT: THERE ARE A TOTAL OF 69 WORDS SUCH AS CHIN AND INCH!

1.

2.

3.

4.

5.

6.

7.

8.

9.

10.

WRITE ANOTHER WORD THAT STARTS WITH THE
LETTERS OF THE WORD ZODIAC. FOR EXAMPLE,
THE WORD ZEBRA ALSO BEGINS WITH THE
LETTER Z.

z-_______________________________________

o-_______________________________________

d-_______________________________________

i-_______________________________________

a-_______________________________________

c-_______________________________________

CHINESE ZODIAC
COLORING & FUN FACTS

* 9 7 8 1 9 8 3 8 3 9 1 6 0 *